A YEAR OF SELF-REFLECTION JOURNAL

A YEAR OF
SELF-REFLECTION
JOURNAL

365 Days of Guided Prompts to Slow Down, Tune In, and Grow

GG RENEE HILL

ROCKRIDGE PRESS

Interior and Cover Designer: Lindsey Dekker
Art Producer: Hannah Dickerson
Editor: Mo Mozuch
Production Editor: Ruth Sakata Corley
Production Manager: Martin Worthington

All illustrations used under license from iStock.com
Author photo courtesy of Tomorrow's Portraits

ISBN: Print 978-1-63807-421-2

R0

This journal belongs to

_____

CONTENTS

Introduction 1

Week 1: Choosing Happiness 4

Week 2: Loving-Kindness 9

Week 3: Growth Mindset 14

Week 4: Life Vision 19

Week 5: Making a Difference 23

Week 6: Home Space 28

Week 7: Breathing Room 32

Week 8: Self-Compassion 37

Week 9: Feel Your Feelings 43

Week 10: Overflowing 49

Week 11: Inner Guidance 54

Week 12: Younger You 59

Week 13: Ideas and Inspiration 64

Week 14: Decisions, Decisions 69

Week 15: Loving Yourself 75

Week 16: Life Changes 80

Week 17: Morning Glory 85

Week 18: Managing Abundance 89

Week 19: Lessons in Gratitude 95

Week 20: Relax and Release 101

Week 21: Body Harmony 106

Week 22: Sleep Well 111

Week 23: Under the Surface 115

Week 24: One with Nature 120

Week 25: Healthy Habits 124

Week 26: Creating Space 128

Week 27: Feed Your Imagination 132

Week 28: Reclaiming Focus 138

Week 29: Staying Active 143

Week 30: The Productivity of Rest 147

Week 31: Finding Forgiveness 151

Week 32: The Soul of Success 156

Week 33: Friendship Matters 160

Week 34: Family Ties 165

Week 35: The Hope in Sadness 169

Week 36: Life Lessons 174

Week 37: Letting Go 179

Week 38: Slowing Down 184

Week 39: People-Pleasing 189

Week 40: Inner Voice 194

Week 41: Grief and Loss 199

Week 42: Beyond Guilt 203

Week 43: Building Courage 207

Week 44: Vulnerability and Healing 212

Week 45: Passion and Purpose 216

Week 46: Sacred Practices 220

Week 47: Embracing Complexity 224

Week 48: Inner Journey 229

Week 49: Mindful Motivation 235

Week 50: More Than Enough 239

Week 51: Everyday Advocacy 244

Week 52: Adventure Awaits 248

A Final Word 253

Resources 254

References 256

"*A self is not something static,
tied up in a pretty parcel and handed
to the child, finished and complete.
A self is always becoming.*"

— MADELEINE L'ENGLE

INTRODUCTION

How often do you take a moment to reflect on your life and look for meaning?

Maybe it's annually on New Year's Day or on your birthday. It could be weekly at church or nightly before you go to bed. You may not make time for self-reflection at all. You wouldn't be alone.

Many of us are so focused on keeping up with our goals and responsibilities that we rarely slow down long enough to process our thoughts, feelings, and actions—certainly not on a daily basis. We prioritize outward productivity and dismiss self-reflection as a waste of time or a luxury at best.

What we don't realize is that reflection gives us the capacity to pause and make conscious choices instead of having automatic reactions to what's going on around us. It allows us to observe the assumptions and judgments we make, consider different perspectives, and find meaning that increases our awareness of our internal and public selves.

We are all affected by outside influences and the pressures of the world around us. Without self-awareness, we are even more vulnerable because we are not tuned into our inner guidance. Research suggests that journaling is a fundamental tool for self-reflection, as it allows us to transform our observations into intentional decisions and actions that align with who we are and who we want to be.

Whether you are a seasoned journal enthusiast or this is your first guided journal, I'm honored that *A Year Of Self Reflection Journal* found its way to you. As a workshop facilitator and creative coach, I've spent the last eight years helping individuals and organizations uncover old stories about who they are and create new narratives that are aligned with their values. My books and workshops center writing as a tool for healing, growth, and advocacy.

It was through journaling that I began to remember who I was before the world told me who I should be.

I was a highly sensitive child with a deep curiosity about life and human nature. Somewhere along the way I stopped valuing myself for who I was and started molding myself into who I thought other people wanted me to be. Journaling was the path I took to come home to myself.

Whether you are seeking a deeper understanding of your character, to heal from pain and loss, or to create an optimistic view of your future, journaling is one of the most effective ways to discover beliefs, patterns, and habits that aren't serving you and open your mind to what's possible.

Within each of us is a powerful capacity to shape our lives by connecting with our values and making conscious choices, but instead many of us simply react to what happens around us, not knowing how to harness this power.

Through daily self-reflection, you can notice how your mind and body react to external circumstances. You can discover—and observe without judgment—what you like, don't like, and want to change. You can allow yourself to dream, visualize, and expand your creative potential.

It's important to note the difference between self-reflection and rumination. Many people experience rumination as loops of thought that keep repeating, that are based in negative thought patterns, and involve replaying painful situations and memories over and over. Through rumination, you assume that you will eventually gain some kind of insight, but you get stuck and go in circles instead of moving forward. Reflection, on the other hand, has everything to do with learning and growing, engaging that energy in productive ways like journaling and other forms of self-care.

BENEFITS OF SELF-REFLECTION

Self-reflection makes it easier to process your emotions and understand why something bothers you. It helps you identify your core values and leverage them to find purpose and courage. The more self-aware you become, the more you grasp the connection between your feelings, thoughts, and actions, which leads to deeper authenticity, decreased stress and anxiety, and healthier relationships and interactions.

In the long-term, self-reflection leads to an increased awareness of what you truly want and what's possible. It broadens your perspective to help you make sense of the world and decide how you want to show up in it. When it comes to your personal and professional development, self-awareness helps you identify limiting beliefs that could be holding you back and preventing your growth.

There is evidence to support the idea that self-reflection through journaling is also beneficial to physical well-being. Research by Dr. James Pennebaker suggests that regular journaling strengthens the immune system and that writing about personal events helps individuals come to terms with their personal experiences, thus reducing the impact of stress on physical health.

THE IMPORTANCE OF DAILY REFLECTION

This journal will guide you through 365 days of writing prompts, hands-on exercises, positive affirmations, and inspirational quotes. Some of the prompts and exercises will be easy for you and others will be challenging. Be patient with yourself and embrace both possibilities. Each week has a theme, with a quote to reflect on or an affirmation to recite out loud on the seventh day. Some exercises will prompt you to write about your experiences in longer form outside of this guided format, perhaps in a separate journal or notebook.

As with any other type of personal growth, committing to self-reflection takes time, patience, and practice. I recommend working through the journal one day at a time, but I also encourage you to find your own rhythm and complete the book in whichever way works best for you.

Journaling is a life-changing practice that we come to rely on more and more as we show up for it each day. While a guided journal practice is a great way to take responsibility for your healing and growth, any ongoing or debilitating feelings of anxiety or depression should be addressed by a medical professional. This book is not a replacement for a therapist, medication, or medical treatment. There is no shame in seeking help or treatment.

The key to self-reflection is compassion. You are not doing this to dig up painful feelings and criticize your past choices. You are doing this to become more intuitive and intentional, to build new habits that align with your values, and to become more centered, peaceful, and happy.

Start with small steps, enjoy the discovery along the way, and build toward consistency. I'm rooting for you!

DAY 1

When you look for external circumstances to make you happy, it's easy to overlook the joy that always lives inside. What makes you feel joyful, even when circumstances aren't going your way?

_____

_____

_____

DAY 2

Describe what it feels like in your body to be in a happy state of mind. Pay particular attention to your throat, chest, and solar plexus areas.

_____

_____

_____

_____

DAY 3

Travel back in time to a happy memory from the past—maybe it's dancing on the beach all night with friends, gardening with your grandmother as a child, or getting your first paycheck. Why does that moment stand out in your memory? Recall the way you felt, then sustain the memory and the feeling for at least 30 seconds. What activity can you plan to recreate that feeling in your life soon? Make a list of ideas.

_____

_____

_____

_____

_____

_____

_____

_____

DAY 4

List five external conditions—people, places, or things—that are a source of happiness in your life.

_____

_____

_____

_____

DAY 5

List five solitary activities that bring you joy and aren't dependent on any external conditions.

_____

_____

_____

_____

_____

DAY 6

Mantras are words or phrases that can be repeated throughout the day when you need a dose of positivity. Make a list of one-sentence mantras that you can say to yourself to tap into your joy at any time. Keep them simple, personally meaningful, and easy to remember. For example, what words might you say to yourself to get back to the feeling you described in your happy memory from Day 3?

_____

_____

_____

_____

_____

_____

_____

_____

_____

_____

DAY 7

"It isn't what you have or who you are or where you are or what you are doing that makes you happy or unhappy. It is what you think about it."

— DALE CARNEGIE

DAY 8

Write about an act of kindness that you witnessed at some point in your life that was meaningful to you. How did it impact the way you treat others?

_____

_____

_____

_____

_____

_____

_____

_____

_____

_____

DAY 9

Think of someone you know who embodies kindness. How do they behave? How do they express their compassion for others?

_____

_____

_____

_____

DAY 10

Reflect on a time when you were judgmental instead of compassionate. How did it make you feel? What did you learn?

_____

_____

_____

_____

_____

DAY 11

Knowing how to be kind to yourself is the first step to creating more kindness in the world. Reflect on what your authentic needs are and what you believe all beings instinctively desire. Some examples include love, freedom, health, and peace. First, in the space below make a word bank of words/phrases that reflect your authentic needs. Then circle the three needs you value the most. Finally, fill in the blanks to create loving-kindness mantras.

AUTHENTIC NEEDS

May I be _____

May I be _____

May I be _____

Example:

May I be loved.

May I be free.

May I be at peace.

DAY 12

Every intention has an effect or consequence. What impact do kindness and compassion have on the condition of society?

_____

_____

DAY 13

The following loving-kindness meditation practice involves reflecting on feelings of goodwill to give rise to positive feelings in the mind and body, and to then share those intentions with the world.

1. Choose a quiet area and sit in a comfortable position with your back straight and eyes closed.

2. Silently repeat the mantras you created on Day 11 : "May I be _____ "; "May I be _____ "; "May I be _____."

3. Pause to sit with how the words make you feel. Repeat as many times as you like.

4. End your practice by saying: "May I and everyone else be peaceful"; "May I and everyone else be happy"; "May I and everyone else be safe."

   Try this exercise daily for one week and write about your experience in a separate notebook or journal.

DAY 14

"Remember there's no such thing as a small act of kindness. Every act creates a ripple with no logical end."

— SCOTT ADAMS

DAY 15

What are you able to do today that you didn't think you would be able to do a year ago?

_____

_____

_____

_____

DAY 16

Reflect on the last time you did something outside of your comfort zone. Describe what happened, including how you felt before and after.

_____

_____

_____

_____

DAY 17

What new opportunities have come out of challenges you've faced? In the table below, create a list of challenges you've faced in the last few years. Next to each challenge, write what you learned, what opportunities developed, and why you are grateful for those experiences.

CHALLENGES	WHAT YOU LEARNED	OPPORTUNITIES THAT DEVELOPED	WHY YOU'RE GRATEFUL

DAY 18

When you were growing up, did you receive positive or negative reinforcement when you tried new things? What words were said to you and how do those words affect you now?

_____

_____

_____

DAY 19

Do you place more value on comfort or growth? Why? In what ways do your actions reflect this priority?

_____

_____

_____

_____

_____

_____

DAY 20

What skill or capability could you pursue this week that would make your personal or professional life easier or more efficient? Write down your thoughts about what has kept you from learning this skill.

_____

_____

_____

_____

_____

_____

Now take at least one of the following action steps:

» Tell someone you trust about your aspiration and ask them to hold you accountable.

» Make a phone call or send an email to someone who can offer guidance.

» Spend one hour researching the topic, taking notes, and mapping out a plan.

DAY 21

---

*"When I step outside of my comfort zone
to follow what inspires me, I grow,
transform, and evolve."*

DAY 22

Do you have dreams for your life that you don't believe can come true? Write down all the doubts that come to mind when you think about bringing your inner visions to life.

_____

_____

_____

DAY 23

Have you ever shared your dreams with anyone? How did they respond? How did their response affect you?

_____

_____

_____

_____

_____

DAY 24

Imagine that your dreams have come true. How would that feel? Write about it in the present tense, using your five senses. For example:

"I am sitting in my home office with natural light shining in the windows. My home is paid for, and I am debt-free. I smell food cooking and I hear the laughter of my family in the background."

Create a picture with words that brings the dream to life and the details into focus.

_____

_____

_____

DAY 25

What thoughts and beliefs would you need to change in order to believe that your dreams are possible?

_____

_____

_____

DAY 26

Reflect on a time when something you wished for came true. What was that experience like? Do you believe the wish came true because of luck, belief, hard work, or perhaps a combination of factors? Explore this below.

_____

_____

_____

_____

DAY 27

Create an inspiration board to capture images and words that reflect the dreams in your mind's eye. You can use a poster board with glue or tape, or a cork board with thumb tacks. You will also need a stack of old magazines.

» Look for images that show what you want to be doing, where you want to live and explore, and accomplishments that are meaningful to you.

» Look for words and phrases that capture the empowerment you want to feel.

» Post everything onto the board in a collage. Be free and creative.

» Hang your collage in a place where you will see it every day.

DAY 28

WEEKLY AFFIRMATION

"I believe that my imagination is powerful and my dreams can become my reality."

DAY 29

What have you experienced or overcome that gives you a unique perspective on life?
Do you ever share your story or this perspective with others? Why or why not?

_____

_____

_____

_____

DAY 30

If you didn't have to think about money and you weren't influenced by people's opinions, how
would you want to make a difference in the world? Why?

_____

_____

_____

_____

DAY 31

What do people often ask you for help with that comes naturally to you and makes you feel purposeful? Describe how it feels to apply yourself this way.

_____

_____

_____

_____

_____

_____

_____

_____

_____

_____

DAY 32

What issues in the world pull at your heartstrings? In the first column, write down the world problems that you wish you could change. In the second column, write down the abilities, talents, strengths, and unique gifts that you possess. In the third column, list ways that your personal qualities in the second column can help solve the problems in the first column.

WORLD PROBLEMS	PERSONAL QUALITIES	HOW YOU CAN HELP
Mental health stigma	Mental illness experience Writing + storytelling Vulnerability	Sharing personal story publicly through writing and storytelling to create awareness

DAY 33

What do you want people to remember about you? How do you want to influence people?

_____

_____

_____

DAY 34

Choose three people that you trust and ask each of them to have a conversation with you about what they perceive your strengths to be. These questions can help frame the discussion:

» *What are my greatest strengths?*

» *What am I good at?*

» *How have my experiences shaped me?*

» *What mistakes have I turned into opportunities?*

Take notes or record these conversations so you can reflect on themes and ideas that reveal themselves.

DAY 35

"Everyone has been made for some particular work, and the desire for that work has been put in every heart."

— RUMI

DAY 36

If you could change anything about your living or workspace to make it more reflective of who you are, what would it be? Use your five senses to describe your ideal space in detail.

_____

_____

_____

_____

DAY 37

What room in your home is your favorite? Why?

_____

_____

_____

_____

DAY 38

Choose an area of your home to clean, organize, or redecorate. Keep in mind the discoveries that you made through Day 36's prompt. Which details that you listed about your ideal space are possible to implement now? Journal about the transformation process.

_____

_____

_____

DAY 39

Make a list of places you like to go for peace of mind. You might say the open road, a garden, or perhaps a gym or a place of worship. How does this environment bring you peace? Can you incorporate some of those characteristics into your home space?

_____

_____

_____

_____

_____

DAY 40

Make a list of places you tend to avoid. What is it about these spaces that makes you want to stay away? What does your response show you about yourself?

_____

_____

_____

_____

DAY 41

Wherever you are right now, take a moment to look around and notice your surroundings. Make a point to observe details that you normally don't notice. Write a description of your environment using your five senses to translate.

» **See:** _____

» **Hear:** _____

» **Smell:** _____

» **Taste:** _____

» **Touch:** _____

DAY 42

WEEKLY AFFIRMATION

"I beautify my life by creating environments that inspire me."

DAY 43

What boundary do you secretly want to set, but you're afraid of disappointing others? It might help to think about what would be liberating to start or stop doing.

_____

_____

_____

_____

DAY 44

How would your mindset and beliefs have to change in order for you to feel worthy and deserving of setting boundaries that serve you?

_____

_____

_____

_____

DAY 45

Take a look at your calendar or your most recent to-do list. Identify one thing that you're expected to do that is not meaningful or fulfilling to you. Write down the steps you can take to alleviate yourself of this responsibility. The first step might be to write a one-sentence statement that declares your freedom to take back your time.

_____

_____

_____

_____

DAY 46

Once you've removed the responsibility from the previous exercise, you will have more breathing room in your life. How can you use that space to nurture your well-being or serve others in a more authentic way?

_____

_____

_____

DAY 47

What boundaries do you already have in place that you struggle to enforce? How do you feel when you don't honor them? Identify the thoughts that go through your mind when you choose to not speak up.

_____

_____

_____

_____

_____

_____

_____

_____

_____

_____

DAY 48

Think of a boundary as a promise that you make to yourself to protect your energy and well-being. Choose a boundary (or promise) that you will honor for the next seven days, no matter how tempted you are to give in. Role-play different scenarios with someone you trust, or practice what you will say in the mirror.

_____

_____

_____

_____

_____

_____

_____

_____

_____

DAY 49

"When I honor my needs and create boundaries that allow me to breathe, I feel more capable and confident."

DAY 50

Think about a time when a loved one was going through a difficult time and they asked you for support. How did you respond?

_____

_____

_____

DAY 51

Now, think about a time when **you** were going through difficulties or feeling bad. How did you support yourself? Were you critical or compassionate? Why do you think that is?

_____

_____

_____

_____

DAY 52

Write down the differences between how you treated the loved one and how you treated yourself. To what extent do you give yourself the same compassion that you give to others?

_____

_____

_____

_____

DAY 53

If the compassionate part of you could speak to the critical part of you, what would it say? In searching for the words, imagine how you would stick up for your best friend in this situation.

_____

_____

_____

_____

_____

DAY 54

Close your eyes, place your hands over your heart, and tune into the rhythm of your heart beating. Breathe in through your nose and out through your mouth as you center yourself in the moment. Meditate on the love you feel for someone you care deeply about. Think about the love a mother feels for her children and how she comforts them when they cry. How does it feel to conjure this love and direct it toward yourself?

_____

_____

_____

_____

_____

_____

_____

_____

_____

_____

DAY 55

Develop a three-part self-care plan for when you are struggling with self-compassion and need comfort, soothing, and validation.

» **Comfort:** What is one thing you can do to self-soothe and meet your emotional needs?

_____

_____

_____

_____

» **Soothe:** What is one physical action you can take to calm yourself and relax your mind and body?

_____

_____

_____

» **Validate:** What is one thing you can say to give yourself permission to feel the way you feel?

_____

_____

_____

_____

_____

_____

_____

_____

_____

_____

_____

DAY 56

"I deserve tenderness, and being gentle with myself makes me stronger."

DAY 57

Name one emotion that you've been having a hard time with lately. How do you feel when you suppress your feelings?

_____

_____

_____

DAY 58

Name one emotion that has been easy for you to express lately. How do you feel when you express yourself authentically?

_____

_____

_____

_____

_____

DAY 59

Think about the last time you were angry. Which of your personal values were not being honored in that situation?

_____

_____

_____

_____

_____

_____

_____

_____

_____

_____

_____

DAY 60

Free writing is a technique that allows you to capture your authentic ideas and thoughts while reducing the likelihood that you'll censor yourself. You simply transcribe your thoughts and let them flow onto the page without stopping until the timer goes off.

1. Take a few deep breaths, quiet your mind and relax.

2. Forget all rules about grammar, punctuation, and sentence structure.

3. Set a timer for 15 minutes and write about any emotional ups and downs you've been experiencing lately.

4. When the time is up, step away for a bit, then come back to read what you wrote and notice what insights come to you.

_____

_____

_____

_____

_____

_____

DAY 61

Do you make most of your decisions with your heart (emotions) or with your mind (logic)? In what ways do you try to balance the two?

_____

_____

_____

_____

_____

_____

_____

_____

_____

_____

DAY 62

What words do you need to hear to feel energized and optimistic? You can give yourself the best pep talks because you know your strengths and weaknesses better than anyone else. Create a video or audio recording of yourself giving a self-directed pep talk that you can watch or listen to when you are feeling down.

1. Talk to yourself in the second person. This allows you to be more objective.

2. Speak specifically to your values, needs, and goals.

3. Use positive language instead of negative. For example, you could say, "Keep moving forward!" instead of, "Stop looking back!"

_____

_____

_____

_____

_____

_____

_____

DAY 63

"Our feelings are our most genuine paths to knowledge."

— AUDRE LORDE

DAY 64

Reflect on a time when you made a difference in someone's life by giving your time, energy, skills, or resources. What did this experience teach you about generosity?

_____

_____

_____

DAY 65

Do personal boundaries allow you to be more or less generous? Explain your answer.

_____

_____

_____

_____

_____

DAY 66

Start a habit of thanking or complimenting someone that you appreciate once a week. It could be a family member, friend, coworker, or acquaintance. It could be a text, email, letter, visit, or phone call. Be realistic and make it easy to keep this promise to yourself by setting a reminder on your phone. Journal about how this habit makes you feel.

_____

_____

_____

_____

_____

_____

_____

_____

_____

_____

DAY 67

What beliefs do you have about giving and generosity? Where do you think those beliefs come from?

_____

_____

_____

_____

DAY 68

What do you have plenty of that you could give away? Think of both tangible and intangible things. Who could benefit from your overflow?

_____

_____

_____

_____

DAY 69

Look at your calendar. When is the next opportunity you have to proactively do something helpful for someone in your life? It doesn't have to be a big or expensive gesture. The key to this exercise is that the idea comes from your desire to give in an authentic way, as opposed to associating giving with obligation. Perhaps you want to treat someone to a coffee or let them pick your brain about a topic you're knowledgeable about. Brainstorm ideas, circle the one that you are most drawn to, and break the task down into simple action steps.

_____

_____

_____

_____

_____

_____

_____

_____

_____

DAY 70

"You give but little when you give of your possessions. It is when you give of yourself that you truly give."

— KAHLIL GIBRAN

DAY 71

If you had to choose one guiding principle to live by, what would it be? Why?

_____

_____

_____

DAY 72

Write the story of why yesterday's guiding principle is number one for you. For example, if your guiding principle is peace of mind, tell a story about how you came to value it. It might help to think about a time in your life when peace of mind was hard to come by.

_____

_____

_____

_____

_____

DAY 73

Your guiding principles and core values reflect your fundamental beliefs. They are like a compass guiding you along the path to who you want to be. They include concepts like love, authenticity, creativity, gratitude, honesty, and leadership. Make a list of your top ten core values.

_____

_____

_____

DAY 74

What are the qualities of the people you look up to and surround yourself with? How do they embody values that you admire?

_____

_____

_____

_____

_____

DAY 75

What core values will be important to actualizing the dream you described on Day 24? Why?

_____

_____

_____

_____

_____

_____

_____

_____

_____

_____

DAY 76

Choose one of your core values and think about how you can bring it to life through mental, emotional, physical, spiritual, professional, and social actions. Write a habit, hobby, activity, or practice that embodies this value.

VALUE:	ACTIVITY
Mental	
Emotional	
Physical	
Spiritual	
Professional	
Social	

DAY 77

"The key to the ability to change is a changeless sense of who you are, what you are about and what you value."

— STEPHEN R. COVEY

DAY 78

Think back to who you were ten years ago. Write down three life lessons you would share with that version of you.

_____

_____

_____

_____

_____

_____

_____

_____

_____

_____

_____

_____

DAY 79

What did you dream of doing as a child? In what ways are those dreams similar to or different from the dreams you have now?

_____

_____

_____

_____

_____

DAY 80

Look at pictures of younger versions of yourself and choose one that you feel particularly connected to. What was inspiring you at the time? What made you feel alive? What creative activities could you make room for in your life now that connect you to this version of yourself?

Make a commitment to spend 30 minutes a week (or any amount of time that works for you) rediscovering your younger self through one of the creative outlets you have in common.

_____

_____

DAY 81

Describe a time when you felt misunderstood as a child. How did you react to this feeling? Do you have a similar reaction to being misunderstood now?

_____

_____

_____

_____

DAY 82

What coping mechanisms helped you survive earlier in life but are no longer useful?

_____

_____

_____

_____

DAY 83

Write a series of positive affirmations that address the struggles of your inner child. For example,

» *You are loved and treasured.*

» *Your feelings matter.*

» *You deserve to speak your truth and take up space.*

» *Nothing you can say or do will make me love you less.*

_____

_____

_____

_____

_____

_____

_____

DAY 84

"Caring for your inner child has a powerful and surprisingly quick result: Do it and the child heals."

— MARTHA BECK

DAY 85

In what ways does your imagination help you manage the tasks and responsibilities of your daily life?

_____

_____

_____

_____

_____

_____

_____

_____

_____

DAY 86

For each task listed, explore ways that you can make these routine processes more creative and suited to your needs:

» **Budgeting your money:**

_____

_____

» **Folding laundry:**

_____

» **Planning your schedule:**

_____

_____

» **Preparing meals:**

_____

DAY 87

What new idea piqued your curiosity this week? Set aside some time to research this idea or topic and take notes here.

_____

_____

_____

_____

_____

DAY 88

Write about the most recent work of art that inspired you. It could be music, literature, visual art, or even a delicious meal. Explain how and why it moved you.

_____

_____

_____

_____

DAY 89

Do you have a creative muse? Who or what is it, and what activities awaken it?

_____

_____

_____

DAY 90

Set aside a few hours to work on a creative project that delights you. It could be building something with your hands, a crafting project, or learning how to play a musical instrument. Use the space below to brainstorm ideas and make a list of the materials and resources you will need.

_____

_____

_____

_____

_____

_____

DAY 91

"My mind constantly produces creative ideas that make my life unique and full of possibility."

DAY 92

How do you handle making big decisions? Who or what do you rely on for guidance?

_____

_____

_____

DAY 93

What is your internal response when a decision you make doesn't give you the result you wanted? How do you usually react and adjust?

_____

_____

_____

_____

DAY 94

Think about a recent decision you made that you had to mull over for a while.

» What choice were you facing?

_____

_____

» What were the possible outcomes?

_____

_____

» What made this decision complex to you? What was at stake?

_____

_____

» What was your decision?

_____

_____

» Did you get the results you wanted?

_____

_____

» What mood were you in when you made your decision?

_____

_____

» Did the decision align with your values?

_____

_____

» How does your answer to the previous question affect how you feel about the outcome?

_____

_____

DAY 95

Most of the time, what do you fear will happen if you make a wrong decision?

_____

_____

_____

_____

DAY 96

What is the most difficult decision you've had to make? Knowing what you know now, would you still make the same decision?

_____

_____

_____

_____

DAY 97

Reflect on a decision you are currently trying to make.

1. At the beginning of the day, state the problem or question out loud and write it down here in your journal.

2. Go about your day as usual, keeping the question open in your mind but without trying to solve it.

3. Throughout the day, write down any helpful signs, impulses, or ideas that reveal themselves to you.

4. Before you go to bed, review your observations from step 3.

5. Repeat this process daily until you come to a decision that aligns with your values and goals.

_____

_____

_____

_____

_____

_____

_____

DAY 98

WEEKLY AFFIRMATION

"When my thoughts, beliefs, and values are in alignment, I make choices that serve my greater good and increase my courage."

DAY 99

What does self-love mean to you? Write down three things you could do today to be more loving and accepting of yourself.

_____

_____

_____

DAY 100

What does self-love look like? Write about someone in your life who exudes self-love and how it shows up in their actions.

_____

_____

_____

_____

_____

DAY 101

Does self-love feel like hard work? Why or why not?

_____

_____

_____

_____

DAY 102

How does your family, culture, and personal background influence your perspective on self-love?

_____

_____

_____

_____

DAY 103

Develop a three-part self-care plan for when you are struggling to give yourself the protection and motivation you deserve.

» **Protection:** What is one thing you can do to put an end to what is hurting you?

_____

_____

» **Provision:** What is one activity or ritual you can do to help you tune into your needs?

_____

_____

_____

» **Motivation:** What is one activity that develops your inner strength and ability to cope?

_____

_____

_____

DAY 104

Write a love letter to yourself to express joy, acceptance, and gratitude for who you are and the life you live. Step outside of yourself and witness your journey with kind eyes. Read the letter often until the tone of the words becomes a natural part of your inner dialogue.

_____

_____

_____

_____

_____

_____

_____

_____

_____

_____

_____

DAY 105

"Most of the shadows of this life are caused by standing in one's own sunshine."

— RALPH WALDO EMERSON

DAY 106

How do you usually react to change? When do you welcome it and when do you resist it?

_____

_____

_____

_____

DAY 107

What is different about your life today compared to 12 months ago?

_____

_____

_____

_____

DAY 108

What changes in the past year have been the hardest to accept? To cultivate positive feelings about these things, notice how shifting your self-talk also shifts your feelings. For each change that you list on the left, complete the prompt on the right.

CHANGE	I AM OPEN TO THIS CHANGE BECAUSE ...

DAY 109

What skills do you have now that you didn't have this time last year? What did you do and how did you have to change to acquire this knowledge?

_____

_____

_____

_____

DAY 110

What life changes—big or small—would be exciting for you right now?

_____

_____

_____

_____

DAY 111

To embrace the idea that change can be beneficial even when it's uncomfortable at first, practice making one small, experimental change. For example, you can try taking a new class at the gym. You can grab a fruit you've never tried before from the grocery store. You might try introducing yourself to people in a new way. In the space below, brainstorm practical ideas, then choose one and take the first step today. Don't forget to come back to write your observations.

_____

_____

_____

_____

_____

_____

_____

_____

DAY 112

"The only way to make sense out of change is to plunge into it, move with it, and join the dance."

— ALAN WATTS

DAY 113

What you do in the morning has a huge impact on the rest of your day. What is your current morning routine?

_____

_____

_____

_____

DAY 114

How do you usually feel when you wake up in the morning? Write down a few of your typical first thoughts.

_____

_____

_____

_____

DAY 115

How do you want to feel in the morning? How would feeling this way empower you throughout the day?

_____

_____

_____

_____

DAY 116

Name five ways that you can center yourself when you wake up feeling stressed. Keep in mind how you want to feel in the morning, then list habits that can help you feel that way.

_____

_____

_____

_____

_____

DAY 117

To become consistent with a new routine, it helps to start as simple as possible and add onto it gradually over time. Choose one of the five things you listed yesterday and build a very small habit around it. Your small habit should incorporate an already existing routine, plus a reward.

    For example, if you would like to start meditating in the morning, commit to sitting on the bed, closing your eyes, and taking five deep breaths every morning when you get out of the shower. That's it. Then reward yourself by turning on your dancing playlist.

    After I _____ (existing routine),

I will _____ (small habit)

+ _____ (reward).

DAY 118

What aspects of your typical morning weigh you down instead of building you up? Maybe when you immediately jump on social media you feel envy or inadequacy; or when you start the day by turning on the news and soon become saddened and overwhelmed. Decide on a new, small boundary to alleviate this influence.

    I will not _____ (unhelpful habit)

until _____ (designate a time of day or a

mood-boosting activity to serve as a prerequisite).

DAY 119

"I'm thankful to start my day with inspired thoughts and actions."

DAY 120

How do you cope with financial stress? Do you think you handle financial situations in a healthy or unhealthy way?

_____

_____

_____

_____

DAY 121

How did your family talk about money when you were growing up? What financial habits and narratives did you pick up from your parents or caregivers?

_____

_____

_____

_____

DAY 122

Check your bank account(s) and look at your financial habits from the last month. To what extent did your spending reflect your values and priorities? Take a few minutes to reflect, then in the first column below make a list of words and phrases that describe how you feel about your decisions. On the right side, write down how you want to feel about your habits.

HOW YOU FEEL	HOW YOU WANT TO FEEL

Are you surprised by any of your observations or responses? How?

_____

_____

_____

_____

_____

_____

_____

_____

_____

_____

_____

DAY 123

What financial accomplishments are you most proud of? What values and habits were needed for you to achieve these things?

_____

_____

_____

DAY 124

If you inherited $50,000 unexpectedly, with the conditions that you cannot spend it on yourself and you have to use it to help others, what would you do with the money? Create an inspiration board or collage to visually show how you would allocate it.

    After doing this exercise, use the space below to reflect on how generosity can improve your relationship with money.

_____

_____

_____

_____

DAY 125

What is your biggest fear when it comes to money? How does this fear show up in your financial decisions?

_____

_____

_____

_____

_____

_____

_____

_____

_____

_____

DAY 126

"All money is a matter of belief."

— ADAM SMITH

DAY 127

Are you surviving or thriving? What do these words mean to you? Explain your response.

_____

_____

_____

DAY 128

What are you most grateful for at this time in your life? Make a list of the people, places, interests, hobbies, and simple pleasures that make you feel abundant. How does making this list affect your mood?

_____

_____

_____

_____

_____

DAY 129

Being honest with yourself can lead to powerful insights. To open your mind to more abundant ways of thinking, write down a list of things that you want to be, do, and have. You can do this exercise daily, weekly, or monthly to help you develop an abundance mindset.

I WANT TO BE...	I WANT TO DO...	I WANT TO HAVE...
in tune with myself, a successful author	travel more, become debt-free	a new car, a healthy relationship

DAY 130

What areas of your life have been challenging your sense of abundance lately? In other words, in what ways do you often feel jealousy, insecurity, or lack?

_____

_____

_____

_____

_____

_____

_____

_____

_____

_____

DAY 131

Choose one area of your life from yesterday and answer the following prompts to connect to the feeling of abundance:

» What is the challenging situation?

_____

» How do you currently feel about it?

_____

» What choice do you have to make?

_____

» How can you grow from making this choice?

_____

_____

_____

_____

DAY 132

Beginner's mind is a mindfulness practice that involves dropping your preconceived ideas and expectations so you can see things with an open mind like a beginner. This practice allows you to turn a mundane activity like washing the dishes into a sensory experience full of wonder and curiosity, thus training your mind to tune into the simple abundance of each day. Note your feelings and observations below.

1. Choose an everyday chore or task, like preparing a meal, and pretend you've never done it before.

2. Pay intimate attention to the details of the task, engaging your five senses in every way.

3. Take your time and move deliberately as if this is the last time you will ever do this and there is something profound to learn from it.

_____

_____

_____

_____

_____

_____

_____

DAY 133

"I am wealthy in ways that go beyond money, and I am worthy of prosperity in all forms."

DAY 134

When you are stressed or burnt out, who or what never fails to make you smile? Why do you think that is?

_____

_____

_____

DAY 135

Think about a real or imaginary place where you can picture yourself relaxing and being at peace. What do you see? Describe it in detail using your five senses.

_____

_____

_____

_____

_____

DAY 136

This body scan meditation promotes physical awareness, stress relief, and relaxation.

1. Lay down or sit in a comfortable position.

2. Take three to four deep belly breaths.

3. Slowly bring your awareness to each part of your body, starting with your feet and making your way up to your head.

4. Notice where you feel tension in your body, and where you feel relaxed.

5. Wherever you find tension, focus on that area, breathe into it, and visualize the discomfort leaving your body through your breath.

6. Write down your observations below.

_____

_____

_____

_____

_____

_____

DAY 137

If you had a friend facing a stressful situation, what would you say to encourage them? Write a note of encouragement below offering advice, wisdom, and love. The next day, come back to look at what you wrote and apply it to your own life.

_____

_____

_____

DAY 138

Write down five sources of stress using the following prompt:

I feel challenged by _____. At the same time, I feel supported

by _____.

_____

_____

_____

_____

_____

DAY 139

Too often, we spend our days racing from one thing to the next. We go from checking emails to making phone calls, to running errands to attending meetings, and we don't give ourselves time to process or catch our breath. Today, practice transitioning calmly from one part of your day to the next at your own pace. Make a note of all the outcomes from this exercise.

_____

_____

_____

_____

_____

_____

_____

_____

DAY 140

*"The greatest weapon against stress
is our ability to choose one thought
over another."*

— WILLIAM JAMES

DAY 141

What promises have you made to your body that you have trouble keeping? What are the possible consequences?

_____

_____

_____

_____

DAY 142

Name one small habit that you can develop to improve your relationship with your body.

_____

_____

_____

_____

DAY 143

Stretching is important and can help you to relax.

1. Gently stretch your body for five to ten minutes, either with a routine you know or one you find online.

2. As you stretch, be aware of how your body works for you.

3. As you breathe, feel your lungs expanding and contracting.

4. Put your hands over your heart and feel the rhythm of your heartbeat.

5. Notice how your muscles and joints feel as you move.

6. When you're done, write a letter to your body thanking it for all the things it allows you to do.

_____

_____

_____

_____

_____

_____

DAY 144

How does your body communicate with you? What do you think it's trying to tell you right now?

_____

_____

_____

_____

DAY 145

If you were in tune and at peace with your body, what bad habits would you have to release in order to honor its needs?

_____

_____

_____

_____

DAY 146

In the space below, write some positive affirmations and quotes about body positivity that you need to hear right now. Transfer your favorites over to sticky notes to post up on your bedroom or bathroom mirror. You can include key words and phrases from the letter you wrote to yourself on Day 143. You can include compliments you have received from other people, or pictures of yourself that you love. Look at them as you prepare yourself in the morning and at bedtime.

DAY 147

WEEKLY AFFIRMATION

"I respect my body for all it does for me, and I honor it with loving thoughts and healthy choices."

DAY 148

Is getting enough sleep important to you? Why or why not? How do you feel when you don't get enough sleep?

_____

_____

_____

_____

DAY 149

Describe how you usually feel at bedtime, physically and emotionally. Does your body feel tense or loose? Are you able to relax easily? Does your mind race or ease quietly into rest?

_____

_____

_____

_____

DAY 150

The 4-7-8 breathing technique can help you relax before going to sleep. To try it, rest the tip of your tongue against the roof of your mouth right behind your top front teeth. Keep your tongue in place throughout the practice as you inhale and exhale. In the cycle of one breath, follow these four steps, then repeat four times.

1. Part your lips and exhale completely through your mouth.
2. Close your lips and inhale slowly through your nose as you count to four in your head.
3. Hold your breath for seven seconds.
4. Exhale from your mouth for eight seconds.

DAY 151

What factors are affecting your nighttime routine and your ability to wind down peacefully at night? Write down what's working and what's not.

_____

_____

_____

_____

DAY 152

What is one small way you can change your evening routine to allow for better rest at night?

_____

_____

DAY 153

Before you go to bed tonight, look in the mirror and answer the following prompts out loud to clear your heart and mind and help you sleep better. The next day, write down a few thoughts about how this practice affected your rest and your mood in the morning.

» What am I grateful for today?

» What parts of today do I need to let go of?

» How do I want to feel tomorrow?

» What are three intentions I have for tomorrow?

_____

_____

_____

DAY 154

"The best bridge between despair and hope is a good night's sleep."

— E. JOSEPH COSSMAN

DAY 155

Are you in touch with your feelings? Do think that you handle your feelings in healthy ways?

_____

_____

DAY 156

In what spaces do you feel comfortable expressing your feelings openly?

_____

_____

In what spaces do you feel uncomfortable expressing your feelings openly?

_____

_____

_____

_____

DAY 157

When you are overwhelmed with conflicting feelings and emotions, you can calm yourself by embracing the duality that you're experiencing.

Sit and breathe slowly to reflect on your emotional landscape in the present moment. What emotions are under the surface? Write them on the left side. Once you've written down all the feelings you can detect at the moment, on the other side write the contradiction to that feeling.

I GIVE MYSELF PERMISSION TO BE...	AND STILL BE...
Sad	Hopeful

When you're done, take it all in and recite the following mantra: *I embrace life's duality in all its many forms.*

DAY 158

What is one emotion you've been having a hard time with lately? Perhaps it's grief, envy, shame, or disappointment. Describe how this emotion has been showing up in your life.

_____

_____

_____

DAY 159

To what extent were you free to express yourself openly as a child? Were you encouraged to talk about your feelings or to suppress them?

_____

_____

_____

_____

_____

DAY 160

In the space below, make a list of people who support you in expressing yourself honestly and who make you feel comfortable being yourself. Next to each name, write about how they make you feel safe. Reach out to one of these people to have an open and vulnerable conversation about something that has been bothering you.

DAY 161

"Negative emotions like loneliness, envy, and guilt have an important role to play in a happy life; they're big, flashing signs that something needs to change."

— GRETCHEN RUBIN

DAY 162

How is the weather where you are right now? How does the weather affect your mood?

_____

_____

_____

DAY 163

When you are outside, which of your five senses is most awakened? Describe how it affects you.

_____

_____

_____

_____

_____

DAY 164

Go for a walk outside and bring your journal with you. Whether you take your walk in a park, on a busy city street, at a festival, or through a quiet neighborhood, find a place to sit down where you can write. Listen to the music of your environment and write down the sounds you hear. Notice how the world around you makes its own music. How does it feel to tune into it? Write about what you see and hear.

_____

_____

_____

_____

DAY 165

If you were one of the four seasons, which one would you be? Why? What characteristics do you identify with that are reflected in that season?

_____

_____

_____

DAY 166

Describe one of your most memorable experiences being outdoors in nature. Where were you? What was happening? Why was it special?

_____

_____

DAY 167

You will need a houseplant for this exercise. If you don't already have one, you can purchase one at the store or ask a friend for a clipping from one of theirs.

　Taking care of houseplants allows you to benefit from nature's life-giving energy in your home.

1. Sit next to your plant and notice the color, texture, and shape of the leaves. Notice the smell and feel of the soil.

2. Look for sprouts of new growth and notice the way they unfurl.

3. Add water, soil, or nutrients as needed.

4. Think loving thoughts and focus on positive feelings as you nurture your plant.

5. How does this exercise affect your mood?

_____

DAY 168

"Everything in nature invites us constantly to be what we are."

— GRETEL EHRLICH

DAY 169

Name a habit or behavior that you know is not serving you. If you made a commitment to go one day without the habit, what could you replace it with?

_____

_____

DAY 170

What is one small habit that you've been wanting to start that will impact your life positively?

_____

_____

What is one bad habit you have that is costing you more than what it is giving you?

_____

_____

_____

DAY 171

Refer to the habit you named on Day 169. Once you decide how you will replace the habit, acquire any necessary materials. For example, if you want to stop having dessert before bed, instead of eliminating it altogether, replace the dessert with a bowl of fruit. Use the space below to create your plan, then come back to record how the one-day experiment goes. What will it take for you to keep this new habit going?

_____

_____

_____

DAY 172

Are you hard on yourself when you engage in habits that you've outgrown? How does this affect your self-esteem?

_____

_____

_____

DAY 173

Who can support you in developing healthier habits? Ideally, what would that support look like?

_____

_____

_____

DAY 174

Develop a reward system to help you build habits that add value to your life. Brainstorm three simple ways that you can celebrate your consistency when you stick to a new habit. Perhaps you reward yourself with permission to wear your fancy underwear after your daily cardio session, or you treat yourself to an at-home facial to celebrate the fact that you've been drinking more water.

_____

_____

_____

_____

DAY 175

"The secret to permanently breaking any bad habit is to love something greater than the habit."

— BRYANT MCGILL

DAY 176

What part of your life is the most cluttered or disorganized? Why do you think that is?

_____

_____

_____

DAY 177

When you consider what it would take to get more organized, what thoughts come to mind?

_____

_____

_____

_____

DAY 178

Getting organized eases feelings of being overwhelmed, heals emotional blocks, and helps you focus. Today, spend ten minutes simplifying and organizing some aspect of your life. You could organize your digital files, clean up your desk, or go through unopened mail. It could be one small corner of your room, or the bathroom counter. By making this a part of your daily routine, you can create a new source of calmness, clarity, and positive energy. Do this a few days this next week and log what you did.

_____

_____

_____

DAY 179

What were you taught about being organized at a young age? How has this teaching helped or hindered you in your adult life?

_____

_____

_____

_____

DAY 180

Reflect on one area of your life that is organized and clutter-free. What's your motivation in that area and how do you maintain it?

_____

_____

_____

DAY 181

Walk around your living space and notice your surroundings. Look at the counters, drawers, and closets. Take stock of how your belongings make you feel. Do you find this tour relaxing or stressful? Why is that?

_____

_____

_____

_____

_____

DAY 182

WEEKLY AFFIRMATION

"As I declutter my life, I open up space to receive the support and clarity that I need."

DAY 183

Where is your favorite place to go for creative inspiration? Whether it's the library or a mountain top, how does this environment move you?

_____

_____

_____

_____

DAY 184

What is your favorite creative outlet? Describe how you feel when you're in the flow of this activity.

_____

_____

_____

_____

DAY 185

Start your day with inspiration. Read, watch, or listen to something uplifting that stimulates you creatively and opens your mind. You might listen to a thought-provoking podcast, read a book on a topic that you're passionate about, or watch an interview of someone that challenges your belief systems and broadens your perspective. How could this practice feed your imagination in a positive way?

_____

_____

_____

_____

_____

_____

_____

_____

_____

_____

DAY 186

Write down 10 creative ideas that seem impossible but inspire your imagination in some way. Don't overthink it. The idea is to allow yourself to dream without limits.

1. _____

2. _____

3. _____

4. _____

5. _____

6. _____

7. _____

8. _____

9. _____

10. _____

DAY 187

What topics would you like to know more about? Have you always wanted to learn more about politics? Perhaps you want to learn how to sew. What are you curious about?

_____

_____

_____

_____

_____

_____

_____

_____

_____

_____

DAY 188

Find a video or documentary online about one of the topics you noted on Day 187 and watch it. When you absorb content that you are genuinely interested in, your mind will be stimulated and ripe with ideas. Writing, doodling, and brainstorming are creative tools that help you process content after you take it in. You can also use mind maps to take notes and connect ideas that you want to explore.

In the space below, doodle or create a collage to capture what you took away from the video. If you're more of a note-taker, you can simply write down your thoughts and key takeaways.

DAY 189

"Creative activity is a type of learning process where the teacher and pupil are located in the same individual."

— ARTHUR KOESTLER

DAY 190

There are so many distractions in the world these days. What boundaries and methods do you have in place to help you stay focused on what you need to do each day?

_____

_____

_____

DAY 191

What is your biggest time management challenge and what impact does it have on your goals and relationships?

_____

_____

_____

_____

DAY 192

Experiment with the ABC method today when you are faced with an interruption, then journal your thoughts afterward.

"A" stands for awareness. You recognize the distraction and realize you have to make a choice.

"B" stands for breath. You breathe deeply and consider your options. Do you allow the distraction or enforce your boundaries?

"C" stands for choice. You consider the situation and your values and make a decision.

   If you choose to enforce your boundaries, the next step is to go back to what you were working on. If you decide to allow the distraction, you can do so knowing that you're making a conscious exception.

DAY 193

Describe someone who you admire for their ability to remain focused. What are their qualities and habits? How can you translate some of these habits into your approach to life?

_____

_____

_____

_____

DAY 194

Are there certain areas of your life where you have no trouble focusing and managing distractions? What's different about those situations?

_____

_____

_____

_____

_____

_____

_____

_____

_____

_____

_____

DAY 195

To improve concentration and focus, try this meditation technique.

1. Sit in a comfortable position and breathe deeply.

2. Silently count from one to ten as you breathe, with the odd numbers on the in-breath, even numbers on the out-breath.

3. After completing one cycle, repeat, but this time only count the odd numbers on the in-breath and suppress the even numbers on the out-breath. In other words, on the out-breath, don't think anything.

4. Repeat one more time.

Was this difficult for you? How so?

_____

_____

_____

_____

_____

_____

DAY 196

"Focus is a matter of deciding what things you're not going to do."

— JOHN CARMACK

DAY 197

What are some of your favorite ways to move your body? Even if it's not something that is part of your life now, reflect on your experiences over the years.

_____

_____

_____

DAY 198

Name one area of physical health you excel in, and one area you would like to improve. Brainstorm ways that you could combine these things in some way.

_____

_____

_____

_____

_____

DAY 199

Try a new sport or exercise routine that you can emotionally connect with in some way. Perhaps you grew up playing basketball and haven't set foot on a court in years. Maybe you love to dance and would like to do it more often because it feels more like fun than hard work. Figure out what fitness style suits you and plan a simple workout routine around this style so you're more likely to stick with it.

DAY 200

What part of your body do you feel most disconnected from? What activities help you become more connected?

_____

_____

_____

_____

_____

_____

_____

DAY 201

How does a lack of movement influence your mood and state of mind?

_____

_____

_____

DAY 202

To be proactive about moving your body more often, set an alarm on your phone to trigger movement breaks at different points in the day. This is a simple way to ensure that you get up from your desk or stop what you're doing periodically to tune into your body and check in with yourself. Remember that small habits done consistently make a big difference in the long run. How can you move your body during these short breaks? Brainstorm ideas below.

_____

_____

_____

_____

_____

DAY 203

"I am in tune with my body's need to move, stretch, and be active."

DAY 204

Do you feel like you have enough energy for the things you want to do? Why do you think that is?

_____

_____

_____

_____

DAY 205

Have you ever been called lazy? What is your instinctive reaction to that word?

_____

_____

_____

_____

DAY 206

Make a list of all the negative ideas, phrases, situations, and cultural norms that you have absorbed about rest. Maybe your work environment celebrates those who work long hours and penalizes those who take their scheduled breaks and leave on time. What influences have shaped your experience?

Secure yourself 30 additional minutes of rest today. That could mean going to bed 30 minutes earlier, sleeping later, or taking two 15-minute power naps. Create a plan that works for you.

_____

_____

_____

DAY 207

Other than rest and relaxation, in what ways do you preserve your energy? How are these methods working for you?

_____

_____

_____

_____

DAY 208

What does it feel like to be burnt out with no relief or rest in sight? Does this way of being improve or dampen your frame of mind? How does this show up in your life?

_____

_____

_____

_____

DAY 209

Plan a day of rest on your calendar. Don't allow anything to be scheduled on that day and ask for support with your responsibilities. On that day, turn off your alarm and sleep in. Spend the day only doing things that relax and recharge you. What will you do that day? Start planning in the space below.

_____

_____

_____

_____

DAY 210

WEEKLY AFFIRMATION

"Rest is productive, and it is safe for me to take breaks."

DAY 211

Are you holding a grudge against anyone? How do you think this grudge affects your life? Write about the details below.

_____

_____

_____

_____

_____

_____

_____

_____

_____

_____

DAY 212

Do you think people who forgive easily are happier? How do you draw the line between being forgiving and being taken advantage of?

_____

_____

_____

_____

_____

_____

_____

_____

_____

_____

_____

DAY 213

Have you ever forgiven yourself for any mistakes or grudges you've been holding over your own head? Create personal mantras based on the prompts below to release the blame you've been holding onto, then read each one aloud to yourself.

» I am letting go of _____.

» I am capable of moving past _____.

» I am trading in my blame and guilt in exchange for _____.

» I have the courage to release _____.

DAY 214

Do you think you are more forgiving toward yourself or toward others? Why?

_____

_____

_____

_____

_____

DAY 215

When you are afraid to forgive someone or yourself, what are you afraid of losing?

_____

_____

_____

_____

DAY 216

Think about the grudge you identified on Day 211 and write a goodbye letter to the discomfort you've been carrying. Consider telling the grudge what you have learned from it and how your life will improve by letting it go.

_____

_____

_____

_____

_____

DAY 217

"The truth is, unless you let go, unless you forgive yourself, unless you forgive the situation, unless you realize that the situation is over, you cannot move forward."

— STEVE MARABOLI

DAY 218

What's your personal definition of success? How has it changed over the years as you've evolved as a person?

_____

_____

_____

_____

DAY 219

Do you consider yourself to be successful? Why or why not?

_____

_____

_____

_____

DAY 220

Many of us limit our definition of success to external or public accomplishments. When we compare ourselves to other people to judge our level of success, we forget what makes us special, what makes us happy, and why.

To stay connected to your own idea of success, offer your time or advice to someone who is a beginner at something that comes naturally to you. How does it feel to share your gifts this way?

_____

_____

_____

DAY 221

What boundaries must you have in place in order to achieve your idea of success? Does the way you currently spend your time and energy allow you to feel successful?

_____

_____

_____

_____

DAY 222

In what ways have your natural gifts created unique opportunities in your life?

_____

_____

_____

DAY 223

Create a work-life balance accountability group with a few friends or coworkers to help each other adhere to shared goals. The objective is to come together periodically (it can be weekly, monthly, quarterly or whatever works for you!) to discuss ideas and challenges, and to help each other brainstorm, solve problems, and encourage each other to stay healthy and manage stress. You get the benefit of constructive feedback, support, and accountability. In the space below, start listing who you might want to include in this group and decide on the steps you need to take to get started.

_____

_____

_____

_____

DAY 224

"Success is not how high you have climbed, but how you make a positive difference to the world."

— ROY T. BENNETT

DAY 225

Name three important qualities that you look for in a friend. Why are these qualities important to you?

_____

_____

_____

DAY 226

Think about one of your closest friends. What makes this relationship special? How has it changed over time?

_____

_____

_____

_____

DAY 227

It's uplifting to see yourself through the eyes of someone who loves you. Ask a friend to join in this activity with you. Make a list of qualities that you admire and appreciate about each other. Next to each quality, write a sentence or two to explain how this makes them special to you.

    Decide what timing works best for both of you and make plans to share your lists with each other.

_____

_____

_____

_____

_____

_____

_____

_____

DAY 228

Which of your friends inspires you to be a better person? Why?

_____

_____

_____

_____

DAY 229

What qualities do you bring to your relationships, both personal and professional?

_____

_____

_____

_____

DAY 230

Ask someone in your life to partner with you for a shared goal. Whether it's meditating once a day for 30 days, reading a book, or drinking a certain amount of water each day, it's easier to do it for yourself when others are doing it with you. Is there someone who may want to join you in the habit you chose for Day 142? Brainstorm ideas below.

_____

_____

_____

_____

_____

_____

_____

_____

_____

DAY 231

WEEKLY AFFIRMATION

"I attract empowering relationships that enrich my life and nourish my individuality."

DAY 232

How do you define family?

_____

_____

_____

DAY 233

What obstacles have you and your family faced? What shared experiences have bonded you together?

_____

_____

_____

_____

DAY 234

How often does your family sit down together for a meal? Plan a meal, whether it's home-cooked or out at a restaurant, with whoever you consider family. When you're sitting around the table, ask everyone to share the peaks (the best parts) and pits (the worst parts) from their day. How did it go? Do you think the conversation starter helped people open up?

_____

_____

_____

DAY 235

What family traditions are most important to you to carry forward? Which traditions do you wish to leave behind? Why?

_____

_____

_____

_____

DAY 236

What does your family most expect from you? What role do you want to play in your family?

_____

_____

_____

DAY 237

How does it feel when you are trying to share a story with someone, and they keep interrupting you? Today, be mindful to practice active listening while talking with loved ones. Active listening involves giving your undivided attention. Instead of thinking about what you'll say next, make eye contact and truly listen. Nod along and repeat back some of their story to show that you're with them. You can use phrases like, "What I'm hearing is…" and, "Tell me more about …" What relationships in your life could benefit from this effort?

_____

_____

_____

_____

DAY 238

WEEKLY AFFIRMATION

"I am grateful for my family and for the lessons that I learn from them."

DAY 239

When was the last time you cried because you were sad? Write what you remember about the situation and describe how you felt at the time.

_____

_____

_____

DAY 240

Sometimes we need to write through our emotions to understand what we're feeling. Does writing about the things that make you sad help you cope? Why or why not?

_____

_____

_____

_____

_____

DAY 241

Many of us view sadness as a weakness, and we suppress it, thinking that it makes us stronger to ignore it. This avoidance prevents us from finding ways to heal and build true resilience. Complete the table below, then try one of the healing actions that you come up with in the third column. How do you feel afterward?

WHAT ARE YOU SAD ABOUT RIGHT NOW?	WHAT SAD THOUGHTS ARE YOU HAVING?	WHAT HEALING ACTION CAN YOU TAKE?
Loss of family member	I miss them. I'll never be happy again. Nothing will ever feel right.	Start a new hobby or project that brings joy and feels like a new beginning.
A failed test or a rejection	I'm a loser. I'm not good enough. Why do I try?	Read or watch something about the upside of disappointment.

DAY 242

Reflect on a time when someone helped you when you were sad. Did you ask for help or did they reach out? How do you feel about receiving help when you're down?

_____

_____

_____

DAY 243

Some people binge television shows when they are sad and others might bury themselves in work. Write down some of the things you do. Do you feel better or worse when you do them?

_____

_____

_____

_____

_____

_____

DAY 244

When we allow it, sadness can be a gateway to creativity. Create a mood board or collage that captures images, color palettes, quotes, song lyrics, prints and/or textures—anything that evokes the feeling of sadness. How does it feel to translate your emotions this way?

_____

_____

_____

_____

_____

_____

_____

_____

_____

_____

_____

DAY 245

WEEKLY AFFIRMATION

"I know that sadness is a feeling that passes like the seasons, and I am open to what it has to teach me."

DAY 246

Think about a recent time when you made a decision that had negative consequences. Describe what you hoped would happen and what actually happened.

_____

_____

_____

_____

DAY 247

Do you believe that mistakes are just mistakes, or do you believe that everything happens for a reason? Where does that belief come from?

_____

_____

_____

_____

DAY 248

What strengths do you have now that you developed through curiosity, trial and error, and persistence? How are you using these strengths?

_____

_____

_____

_____

DAY 249

Write a thank you note to your past self for being brave in the face of uncertainty and putting one foot in front of the other to get you to this point.

_____

_____

_____

_____

DAY 250

It's easy to be thankful for positive experiences, but it's also important to recognize and be thankful for positive outcomes that come from negative experiences.

Complete the table below with three negative experiences or mistakes that you've faced in the past that taught you valuable lessons. How are you grateful for these challenges now?

NEGATIVE EXPERIENCE	POSITIVE OUTCOME	LIFE LESSON LEARNED
I mismanaged my money, fell into debt, and suffered from anxiety.	I took steps to educate myself about mental health and finances. I can share my experience and end this generational pattern.	I learned that my financial distress was really an emotional issue and I learned how to consciously manage my emotions and my finances.

DAY 251

An inspiring visualization technique is to create a "goal picture" or image in your mind of yourself achieving a goal. Visualization can seem strange at first if you've never tried it before, but it's really nothing more than using your mind to picture a desired outcome. This exercise involves recalling a "goal picture" from the past to evoke feelings of confidence and capability.

1. Think of different versions of yourself and all the times you have fallen down and gotten back up.

2. What did the getting up look like? Maybe you picture yourself walking across the graduation stage, after the trials and tribulations that came with that journey. Maybe you picture yourself mending the relationship with your parents after years of estrangement.

How does this visualization affect your feelings about the future?

_____

_____

_____

_____

_____

_____

DAY 252

"I trust myself to reroute when I've chosen the wrong path, and I'm thankful for the lessons I learn along the way."

DAY 253

What does letting go mean to you? What makes it hard to let go? When is it easy?

_____

_____

_____

_____

DAY 254

What has been the hardest thing you have had to let go of in the past? Maybe it was a person, place, belief, idea, or dream. What changed in your life as a result of letting go?

_____

_____

_____

_____

DAY 255

Bring your attention to a specific negative belief that you want to release. Read the following affirmation aloud as many times as you need to for it to sink in, then close your eyes and meditate on it for five minutes, keeping that negative belief in mind. Write your thoughts and feelings afterward.

I am letting go. I am creating space for abundance in my life by releasing what no longer serves me. I am thankful for all that I have, all that I have lost, and all that life has taught me. I embrace my journey with an open heart and open mind.

_____

_____

_____

_____

_____

_____

_____

_____

_____

DAY 256

Think of a place that was special to you when you were younger that is no longer there. How do you hold on to what this place meant to you now that it's gone?

_____

_____

_____

_____

DAY 257

Is there something in your life right now that you need to let go of because it's holding you back? Are you ready to let go? Why or why not?

_____

_____

_____

_____

DAY 258

For this letting go ritual, grab a loose piece of paper and write down every worry, grudge, regret, or painful thought that comes to mind. When you're done, shred, burn or tear the piece of paper up into little pieces. If you live near the water, release the shredded paper into the water or release it into the wind. Journal below about what this act symbolizes and how it helps you let go.

_____

_____

_____

_____

_____

_____

_____

_____

_____

_____

DAY 259

"Some of us think holding on makes us strong, but sometimes it is letting go."

— HERMANN HESSE

DAY 260

Look at your calendar or schedule for this month. Are you satisfied with the amount of free time that you have between obligations? Why or why not?

_____

_____

_____

DAY 261

What would your typical day look like if there were no expectations or responsibilities to tend to and money was not an issue?

_____

_____

_____

_____

_____

DAY 262

Slow living is a lifestyle that embraces intentionality and savoring the minutes of each day instead of rushing through them. To practice this, make yourself a hot drink. Start by choosing a cup or container that you love and a drink based on how you want to feel; perhaps chamomile tea for calmness or coffee for alertness. Take a sip and hold it in your mouth before you swallow it. Notice the temperature, taste, and smell. As you swallow, feel it running down your throat. How does it feel to slow down this way?

_____

_____

_____

_____

DAY 263

When do you feel most rushed, stressed, and overwhelmed? What areas of your life could benefit from a slower pace?

_____

_____

_____

DAY 264

In your opinion, what's the difference between a busy life and a full life?

_____

_____

_____

_____

_____

_____

_____

_____

_____

_____

_____

DAY 265

Too often, people prioritize busyness and productivity over self-care, which leads to stressful lifestyles and mental and physical health problems. To become more intentional about the pace of your life, it's important to be conscious of how much societal narratives are affecting your beliefs and behaviors. For each phrase below, write what you actually believe or have found to be true. Think about perceptions you've picked up from your family, culture, and/or society, and if these perceptions align with your unique values. Then brainstorm a self-care action that might help you manage and complete one in the next week.

WHAT YOU'VE BEEN TAUGHT OR PICKED UP FROM THE WORLD	WHAT YOU ACTUALLY BELIEVE OR HAVE FOUND TO BE TRUE	SELF-CARE ACTION THAT MIGHT HELP
The more you hustle, the better your life will be. You can rest later.		
If you're not always involved, you'll miss something important or become irrelevant.		
If you don't move fast enough, you will get left behind.		

DAY 266

"I schedule my life so I can experience it deeply and create a pace that is empowering for me."

DAY 267

Does the desire to have other people's approval distract you from doing what is best for you? Write down a few examples of how this shows up in your life.

_____

_____

_____

_____

DAY 268

Have you made any big decisions about your education, career, or life path based on other people's expectations? Is there any part of you that wishes you'd chosen differently?

_____

_____

_____

DAY 269

What validation do you tend to seek from other people? Maybe you want to be perceived as kind, smart, successful, or generous. Your answer to this will show you some of your core values.

_____

_____

_____

_____

_____

_____

_____

_____

_____

_____

DAY 270

When you take the time to do things that are meaningful to you on a regular basis, fulfillment and self-affirmation help you detach from the need for validation from others. Think about ways you can honor one of the values you listed yesterday in your own autonomous way. For instance, if you value generosity, what's one way you can be generous without betraying yourself or sacrificing your needs? Use the table below to guide you.

VALUE:	
Ways that I am seeking this value through people-pleasing	**Ways that I can honor this value without sacrificing my needs**

DAY 271

When you put other people's needs above your own, how does that affect your self-esteem?

_____

_____

DAY 272

Your intuition speaks to you through feelings, and the more you cultivate awareness, the more perceptive you become to its guidance. Do a mindful body scan to observe how you feel when you are presented with a choice between being true to yourself or pleasing someone else. How does it feel in your body? Look at the examples you provided on Day 267. Do you feel light or heavy reading your responses? How do your head, heart, and gut feel when you go against yourself? Take notes to describe your feelings.

_____

_____

_____

_____

_____

DAY 273

WEEKLY AFFIRMATION

"When I know that what other people think of me does not define me, I set myself free to be my authentic self."

DAY 274

We can't bully ourselves into self-love. Does negative self-talk ever keep you from feeling good about yourself? What does your inner critic (the critical voice inside your head) say to you?

_____

_____

_____

_____

DAY 275

How often do you question what your inner critic says? What do you think would happen if you stopped paying attention to it?

_____

_____

_____

_____

DAY 276

Calming that scared inner voice changes the relationship you have with yourself, eventually easing the tone of your thoughts from critical to compassionate.

1. To practice this, set a timer for five minutes.

2. Sit still with your eyes closed, breathing deeply into your belly and out through your mouth.

3. On the in-breath, imagine that you are breathing in **judgment and criticism**. On the out-breath, imagine that you are breathing out **love and compassion**.

Describe how you feel after trying this.

_____

_____

_____

_____

_____

_____

_____

DAY 277

Practice being kind to yourself. What are your greatest strengths and gifts? Write a gratitude list focusing on the qualities you love about yourself. Don't be shy!

_____

_____

_____

_____

DAY 278

For each critical thought that you listed on Day 274, write a counter statement with a positive tone. For example, instead of, "You'll never make it," change that to, "You're on your way, keep going."

_____

_____

_____

_____

DAY 279

Write a short pep talk to yourself on a small card or sticky note and leave it somewhere so you can find it later, perhaps in a book you plan on reading soon or in a bag you're not currently using. Write the encouragement from the perspective of someone who loves and admires you. What would your best friend say to you if you were being hard on yourself?

_____

_____

_____

_____

_____

_____

_____

_____

_____

DAY 280

WEEKLY AFFIRMATION

"I love and accept myself.
I am my own best friend."

DAY 281

You experience grief when you lose something you valued. It could be a person, a job, a place, an object, or even a time in your life. What are you grieving right now?

_____

_____

_____

_____

DAY 282

Look at the list of the things that you are grieving from Day 281. Which one is affecting you the most right now? How has your life changed since this loss?

_____

_____

_____

_____

DAY 283

Create a ritual to help you process grief in a specific way that honors your connection with the subject of your loss. You could visit a special place on certain days or write a letter to someone you lost each month. You could create a memory book dedicated to what you lost and spend time working on it and looking through it once a week. Keep it simple and doable. What ritual could you create to honor your loss?

_____

_____

_____

DAY 284

Grief encompasses many different emotions. You might experience guilt or regret over how you treated what you lost before it was gone. You might feel sadness, anger, or relief. What feelings accompany your grief?

_____

_____

_____

_____

DAY 285

Which of the feelings you listed on Day 284 do you want to keep, and which ones do you want to leave behind? What makes the ones you keep valuable to you?

_____

_____

_____

DAY 286

It's important to hold space for joy as we move through the stages of grief. Choose one small thing to look forward to tomorrow that will bring you joy or inspire feelings of hope. You could wear the new dress that's been sitting in your closet or make a reservation to go to a new place for lunch. If you're feeling social, maybe you could plan to call someone who shares this loss, so you can walk down memory lane together and remember good times. Write about how this activity goes.

_____

_____

_____

_____

DAY 287

"What we once enjoyed and deeply loved we can never lose, for all that we love deeply becomes a part of us."

— HELEN KELLER

DAY 288

Do you feel guilty about anything right now? It could be as simple as taking time away from loved ones to journal or as big as making a mistake that hurts someone else. How are you coping with the guilt?

_____

_____

_____

DAY 289

Turn the situation from Day 288 around. How would you feel if the other person did the same thing you did? Would you feel the same way that you feel about yourself? Why or why not?

_____

_____

_____

DAY 290

If you are feeling blocked by guilt, it can be helpful to see the bigger picture. Sometimes wrongs can be imagined, and we take responsibility for things that are outside of our control. Speak to someone you trust about the situation and ask for a different perspective. Make it clear that you are asking because you want to heal and grow from the situation, not because you are looking for someone else to blame. Write down any gems from the conversation that are helpful.

_____

_____

_____

DAY 291

In what ways does guilt have a negative impact on your sense of well-being? How does it affect your self-confidence?

_____

_____

_____

_____

DAY 292

In what ways can guilt have a positive effect on your life? What can you learn about yourself and how does it call you to become more self-aware?

_____

_____

_____

_____

_____

_____

DAY 293

On a separate piece of paper, write a letter to a person or situation that brings up feelings of guilt. The intention is not to send the letter, but to get the feelings out of your body and onto the page. Do you need to apologize? Are there things you need to say that you're scared to say out loud? Perhaps you want to share your side of the story. Depending on the situation, you may want to release responsibility or establish a boundary. See what this exploration reveals to you.

DAY 294

WEEKLY AFFIRMATION

"I gently release guilt and regret so I can move forward with peace of mind and compassion."

DAY 295

Write about how your views of courage were shaped. Who did you look up to for their courage when you were a child? What were their qualities?

_____

_____

_____

_____

DAY 296

What do you picture when you think of courage now? What images and visions come to your mind when you think of courageous people?

_____

_____

_____

_____

DAY 297

Courage is doing what feels right in spite of the presence of fear. You can show courage in big and small ways each day like asking for a raise, sticking up for someone who is being mistreated, or even getting up on a stage in front of an audience to share a talent.

Complete the following table to reflect on different aspects of your life and how you show courage each day.

	EVERY DAY, I AM AFRAID OF . . .	EVERY DAY, I SHOW COURAGE BY . . .
Physical		
Emotional		
Social		
Creative		
Spiritual		
Professional		

DAY 298

Other than yourself, who do you want to be courageous for? Who could your courage help?

_____

_____

_____

_____

DAY 299

Think about a desire that you have for your life. Is what you want worth getting over any fears you may have about getting there? Why or why not?

_____

_____

_____

_____

DAY 300

To strengthen your courage muscles, pursue an act of courage that you've been putting off. You could sign up for a marathon, take a class you've been curious about, or make a phone call that you've been dreading. Choose something that has been weighing on your mind, so you can feel the weight begin to lift when you take that first step. Journal about the process and the emotions you go through.

_____

_____

_____

_____

_____

_____

_____

_____

_____

_____

DAY 301

"Courage is not simply one of the virtues,
but the form of every virtue at the
testing point."

— C. S. LEWIS

DAY 302

When have you felt most vulnerable in your life? Was it a positive or negative experience?

_____

_____

_____

_____

DAY 303

How do you react to emotional vulnerability in others? Does it make you uncomfortable or does it draw you in?

_____

_____

_____

_____

DAY 304

For this word association exercise, start a list of words on a separate paper with "vulnerability" at the top. Under it, write the next word that comes to mind. Next, write the next word that comes to mind and keep going until no more words come to mind. When you're done, observe your list and any themes or patterns that you see. What can you learn about yourself from this list?

_____

_____

_____

DAY 305

In what spaces, relationships, and situations do you feel safe to let your guard down and be your true self? In what spaces does this feel unsafe? For what reasons?

_____

_____

_____

_____

DAY 306

What are your biggest concerns about being vulnerable about your dreams, hopes, fears, and disappointments? On the other hand, what could you possibly gain from it?

_____

_____

DAY 307

When you want to express a part of yourself that you never have before, sometimes you need to create the ideal conditions to feel safe to do so. Invite a few people to a storytelling night, either online or in person. The idea is to normalize vulnerability and truth telling by creating a soft place for your truths to land. If that's too much, choose one person to confide in or share a side of yourself with that you don't broadly share. Journal about the experience.

_____

_____

_____

_____

DAY 308

"When I own my truth and express myself authentically, vulnerability empowers me and brings more fulfillment into my life."

DAY 309

What do people often tell you that you're good at or ask you for help with? How do you feel when they say these things?

_____

_____

_____

DAY 310

What do you love to do that doesn't feel like work and makes you feel good inside? Maybe you like to work with your hands, listen to people's problems, work with numbers, or decorate people's spaces. Make a list below.

_____

_____

_____

DAY 311

What have you dreamed of being or doing that relates to your responses from the last two days but feels out of reach? What excites you about this dream and what holds you back?

_____

_____

_____

_____

DAY 312

What qualities, gifts, and strengths do you have that you want to offer to the world? What does the world need that you could lend your talents to in some way?

_____

_____

_____

_____

DAY 313

Visualize a day-in-the-life where you are able to indulge in your passions each day, including what you're good at and what you love to do, in a way that the world needs and will pay you for. What kinds of appointments, projects, and meetings are on your schedule for that day? Are you working alone or with a group? How do you feel about the work you're doing? Sketch out the scene in the space below and label the key elements.

DAY 314

Spend an hour (or more, if you can!) indulging in an activity that you love to do but haven't done in a long time. After the session, journal about how it felt, then create a plan for dedicating more time for this activity in your schedule. Revisit Day 310 for inspiration if you need it.

_____

_____

_____

DAY 315

"The things you are passionate about are not random, they are your calling."

— FABIENNE FREDRICKSON

DAY 316

Do you consider yourself to be a spiritual person? How does spirituality or faith show up in your daily life through your habits and practices?

_____

_____

_____

DAY 317

What people, figures, or ideas have had the biggest impact on your spiritual life? When have you felt most connected to your spirituality?

_____

_____

_____

_____

_____

DAY 318

Today, go out of your way to be kind and helpful to the people you interact with throughout the day. For example, instead of greeting the security guard at work with nod, say, "Good morning, how are you?" and actually wait for a response. If you notice someone you work with looking down or stressed, ask them if they're okay.

How does that feel? How do people react to you? Do you believe that this is a form of spirituality? Why or why not? At the end of the day, journal your observations about this experiment.

_____

_____

_____

_____

DAY 319

What resources do you use to make sense of life and look for wisdom?

_____

_____

DAY 320

What are the main guiding principles that make up your spiritual practice? If you don't consider yourself to be spiritual, where do your guiding principles come from?

_____

_____

_____

_____

DAY 321

Escape from your daily routine to spend some time in nature. Go on a hike, walk along the beach, or just spend some time in a park or your own backyard. Regard everything you see with fresh eyes and wonder, taking in the sights, sounds, and sensations as if it were the first time. Write about the extent to which this experience makes you feel connected to something bigger than yourself.

_____

_____

_____

DAY 322

*"You have to grow from the inside out.
None can teach you, none can make
you spiritual. There is no other teacher
but your own soul."*

— SWAMI VIVEKANANDA

DAY 323

What are the different roles you play in your life? Do you feel fully expressed in these roles or do you hold pieces of yourself back? If so, how?

_____

_____

_____

DAY 324

Do the needs of different roles in your life ever cause you to feel in conflict with yourself? How? For example, your roles at work may conflict with your roles in your family.

_____

_____

_____

_____

DAY 325

Complete the table below to get clear on what actions you can take to embody your many roles in mindful and empowered ways.

I AM ...	I AM ALSO ...	I EMBODY BOTH BY ...
A passionate writer	A dedicated mother	Communicating my needs, setting boundaries on my time and energy, and trusting my intuition

DAY 326

How would you describe your authentic self? In what ways would you like to bring more of your authentic self into your various roles in life?

_____

_____

_____

_____

DAY 327

What is one thing missing from your life that would make your outer world feel more like a reflection of your inner world? Is it attainable? Why or why not?

_____

_____

_____

_____

_____

DAY 328

When life gets complicated, you can calm yourself at any time by stimulating the vagus nerve, the longest cranial nerve of the human body. It has several roles, including calming you down and reducing the cortisol-producing stress response of fight-or-flight. One way you can strengthen the vagus nerve is by humming or singing. Choose songs you love to sing that make you feel good. Have a private concert while driving in your car or taking a shower for at least three to five minutes, once or twice a day for the next week. How does this affect your mood?

_____

_____

_____

_____

_____

_____

_____

_____

DAY 329

WEEKLY AFFIRMATION

"I embrace the many layers of complexity that make me who I am."

DAY 330

Are you aware of any patterns or cycles in your life that are keeping you stuck? For example, maybe you keep attracting people in your life that drain you. Explore this idea.

_____

_____

_____

DAY 331

Do you ever struggle to sit with yourself, listen to your thoughts, and acknowledge your darker emotions? What do you normally do to distract yourself?

_____

_____

_____

_____

_____

DAY 332

Stand at the mirror and look at yourself with kind eyes. Does this feel uncomfortable? Stay with your reflection and be gentle with yourself through the discomfort. What are your eyes most drawn to? What thoughts go through your mind as you silently observe yourself? Observe the presence of your inner critic and welcome it. Stay with this exercise for five full minutes to develop deeper inner strength and awareness, and to more effectively manage the intensity of your emotions without running away from them.

DAY 333

Do you trust your intuition to provide ideas and impulses to guide you through confusing times? What makes it hard to do this?

_____

_____

_____

_____

_____

_____

_____

DAY 334

What do you usually do to work through confusion and inertia? Is it helpful?

_____

_____

_____

_____

_____

_____

_____

_____

_____

_____

_____

_____

DAY 335

Start an intuition log to keep track of signals, ideas, and impulses that you observe when you are seeking guidance. Use the table below to capture your observations. For each issue, start by filling out the first column and then stepping away. As you go through your daily life, look out for messages and signs that speak to your question and come back to document them here.

WHAT ARE YOU SEEKING GUIDANCE ABOUT?	WHAT SIGNALS, IDEAS, AND IMPULSES HAVE YOU NOTICED?	WHAT MEANING CAN YOU GIVE TO THESE SIGNS?
Whether I should take a job offer that pays well but will take a lot of time away from my main passion: writing.	Conversations about work with friends brought fresh insights. Stomach felt tight when thinking about taking the job offer; a sense of dread. Tried to visualize, but couldn't see myself doing the job and being content.	After several days, I felt certain that this was not the right opportunity for me because my heart and mind did not feel aligned with it.

WHAT ARE YOU SEEKING GUIDANCE ABOUT?	WHAT SIGNALS, IDEAS, AND IMPULSES HAVE YOU NOTICED?	WHAT MEANING CAN YOU GIVE TO THESE SIGNS?

DAY 336

"I am committed to discovering who I am and who I can become when I believe in myself."

DAY 337

What recent accomplishment are you proud of right now? Anything that you motivated yourself to achieve works! It could be something like cutting back on sugar in your diet or improving your grade in a class.

_____

_____

_____

DAY 338

What qualities did you leverage in order to accomplish the goal from Day 337? Where did your motivation come from?

_____

_____

_____

_____

DAY 339

Reflect on a goal you have for your life right now that requires discipline and motivation. Fill out the table below to take stock of the tasks that you consider to be easy and the tasks that you know you'll have to force yourself to do. Develop a plan to partner the easy tasks with difficult tasks to create momentum and progress. After you list all the tasks you know of in the designated columns, draw lines to connect a task from the easy side and pair it with a task from the hard side.

GOAL	TASKS THAT ARE EASY TO DO	TASKS THAT YOU HAVE TO FORCE YOURSELF TO DO
Start a blog or website	Purchase the domain	Come up with a name to capture the idea

DAY 340

What is your usual recourse when you need to do something that you don't feel motivated to do? Are you honest with yourself or do you talk yourself out of it?

_____

_____

DAY 341

Reflect on the accomplishment you shared on Day 337. What was the reason behind wanting to achieve that goal? How did that reason affect your motivation?

_____

_____

DAY 342

Apply the five-minute rule to one of your goals. Commit to working on a task that you're not motivated to do for at least five minutes each day. You could use that five minutes to make a phone call, fill out a form, or watch a tutorial. This is an accessible and effective way to make progress without feeling overwhelmed.

DAY 343

WEEKLY AFFIRMATION

"I acknowledge the progress in my baby steps and celebrate my efforts."

DAY 344

Do you compare yourself with other people? How do your comparisons affect the way you view yourself and the way you show up in the world?

_____

_____

_____

_____

_____

_____

_____

_____

_____

_____

DAY 345

What do you think it means when you are jealous or envious of someone? What does it tell you about your own desires?

_____

_____

_____

_____

_____

_____

DAY 346

Go through your social media accounts and unfollow anyone that triggers you to feel that your life and who you are is not enough. Only follow people that inspire you. If you're not on social media, think about how you can create distance between yourself and anyone in your life that you feel compelled to compete with, at least until you reach a point where you are more content in your own skin and on your own path.

DAY 347

There is a common sentiment that you are only in competition with yourself. Do you agree with that? Why or why not?

_____

_____

_____

_____

DAY 348

Consider these questions with compassion and honesty: Why is it that you are jealous of some people and inspired by others? What makes the difference for you?

_____

_____

_____

_____

_____

DAY 349

Use your imagination. Find a place where you can sit and people watch. Pick a stranger that you feel inclined to compare yourself to or make a judgment about and write their story. Where did they come from? What are their hopes, background, dreams, and fears? What have they had to overcome? Create a fictional story to help you embrace the idea that you can't judge a book by its cover and that we all have stories beyond what people can see.

_____

_____

_____

_____

_____

_____

_____

_____

_____

_____

DAY 350

"Comparison is an act of violence against the self."

— IYANLA VANZANT

DAY 351

What is the number one world or community problem that you would like to help solve?

_____

_____

_____

_____

DAY 352

What is one small thing you can do today to help, spread awareness, or advocate right from your home?

_____

_____

_____

_____

DAY 353

Research service opportunities and find a way to get involved with a cause you care about. Make sure that you feel intimately connected to this cause and participate in a way that honors your unique needs and qualities. If you're a great cook, perhaps you want to cook meals for the sick and shut-in at your church. If you enjoy working with kids, maybe you want to volunteer to read to children at the library. Take the first step this week and reflect on how you can make this a regular part of your life.

_____

_____

_____

DAY 354

Do you believe that one person's actions have an impact on the rest of the world? Why do you feel this way? How does this affect the way you choose to live?

_____

_____

_____

_____

DAY 355

What group of people do you feel that you can help the most based on your gifts, strengths, and experiences? Why?

_____

_____

_____

DAY 356

What story can you tell about yourself to bring attention to the cause you care about? Write about your personal connection to it. You don't have to share your story publicly, but by writing it you will become clear on why it's important to you. If you feel inclined, you can share your story on social media, at a community meeting, or in some other forum. In what ways could this add another layer of purpose to your life?

_____

_____

_____

_____

DAY 357

"I use both my strengths and my struggles to help people and contribute to the world around me."

DAY 358

Do you consider yourself to be an adventurous person? Why or why not?

_____

_____

_____

_____

_____

DAY 359

What legacy do you want to leave behind? Why is this important to you?

_____

_____

_____

_____

DAY 360

Draw a timeline of your life so far. In the space below, start with birth and mark off the seasons of your life along the timeline. You can use ten-year increments, or any other markers you want, like cities you lived in or jobs that you had. Mark the timeline with significant events, turning points, and life changes—any events that had a significant impact on you.

DAY 361

Write about the last adventure you took. An adventure could be taking a new route to work, starting a new job, or traveling across the world—whatever it means to you!

_____

_____

_____

_____

DAY 362

What is one thing you've always wanted to do in your life that you haven't done yet? Do you have a plan?

_____

_____

_____

_____

_____

DAY 363

Create a treasure box to start collecting items, quotes, clippings, photos, and anything else that reminds you of adventures you've taken or adventures you want to take. Similar to a vision board, this is a great way to get in touch with the feelings that adventure brings and to keep your mind open to ideas and opportunities.

DAY 364

How can you find adventure today without even leaving your home?

_____

_____

_____

_____

_____

_____

_____

DAY 365

WEEKLY AFFIRMATION

---

*"Each day I open my heart
to receive the wisdom, joy, and
abundance that life has to offer."*

A Final Word

What more can I learn about myself?

This is the question you will continually ask yourself as you make self-reflection an indispensable part of your self-care strategy and approach to life.

Keep the following tips in mind as you continue your journey:

» **Believe in yourself.** View challenging situations as experiences and not problems. When you get stuck in a cycle or pattern, imagine that your mind is being stretched and you are discovering new pathways that make you more discerning and resilient.

» **Be kind to yourself.** That means don't speak negatively about who you are or what you want. Let go of the habits of criticism, comparison, and judgment. When you entertain thoughts that you aren't good enough, or when you keep affirming that you are stuck or unhappy, you hold yourself in resistance to what you really want.

» **Discover yourself.** Do the self-reflection work to discover what you want, set goals, and take steps to reach them. Be motivated by the evolution of your own life and take action based on what inspires your mind, body, and soul—regardless of what anyone else thinks.

» **Stretch yourself.** Trust your curiosity as much as your current abilities. Feeding your curiosity keeps your creativity engaged and excited.

I hope you will commit to self-reflection through journaling as a lifelong practice so you can benefit from the unlimited discovery that it offers.

RESOURCES

To learn more about the power of self-reflection, authentic expression, mindset, and values, the following resources have been instrumental in my journey and I believe they will serve you as well.

Books

The Artist's Way by Julia Cameron

Atomic Habits by James Clear

The Gifts of Imperfection by Brené Brown

Lovingkindness by Sharon Salzberg

Mindset by Carol S. Dweck

Question Your Life by Gregg Krech

Year of Yes by Shonda Rhimes

Blogs & Websites

Calm: Calm.com

James Clear: JamesClear.com

Journal Smarter: JournalSmarter.com

Mind Body Green: MindBodyGreen.com

Shine: TheShineApp.com

Tiny Buddha: TinyBuddha.com

Womaze: Womaze.com

Zen Habits: ZenHabits.net

Podcasts

The BeFree Project: BeFreeProject.com/podcast

Behind the Brilliance: BehindtheBrilliance.com

Happier: GretchenRubin.com/podcasts

Jay Shetty: JayShetty.me/podcast

New Growth with Nikki Walton: BeHereNowNetwork.com/category/nikki-walton

The School of Greatness: LewisHowes.com/sogpodcast

She's Beauty and the Beast: ShesBeautyandtheBeast.com/podcast

REFERENCES

Chowdhury, Madhuleena Roy, PhD. "What is Loving-Kindness Meditation?" Positive Psychology. March 12, 2021. PositivePsychology.com/loving-kindness-meditation.

Fogg, BJ, PhD. *Tiny Habits: The Small Changes That Change Everything.* Boston: Houghton Mifflin Harcourt, 2020.

Gotter, Ana. "What Is the 4-7-8 Breathing Technique?" Healthline. Last Updated: April 20, 2018. Healthline.com/health/4-7-8-breathing.

Metivier, Anthony. "How to Meditate for Concentration and Focus: A Simple Guide." Magnetic Memory Method. February 19, 2021. MagneticMemoryMethod.com/how-to-meditate-for-concentration.

Scott, Elizabeth, MS. "Body Scan Meditation." Verywell Mind. March 6, 2020. VerywellMind.com/body-scan-meditation-why-and-how-3144782.

Selva, Joaquín, Bc.S. "Albert Ellis' ABC Model in the Cognitive Behavioral Therapy Spotlight." Positive Psychology. February 17, 2021. PositivePsychology.com/albert-ellis-abc-model-rebt-cbt.

ACKNOWLEDGMENTS

I'm eternally grateful for the love and support I've received through this creative journey. I am so thankful to do this work.

Special thanks to the love of my life for believing in me and making sacrifices for our family when I wanted to change careers and become a writer eight years ago.

To my three heartbeats, for inspiring me to be brave, find my voice, and leave a creative legacy.

To my extended family, and friends who are family, thank you for the sisterhood, togetherness, laughter, and support through the years.

To my tribe of peers, colleagues, mentors, and readers that I've collected over the years, thank you for inspiring me, teaching me, and blessing me with opportunities to commune with you and serve.

To Callisto, thank you for the platform to share my passion and help others heal and thrive through writing.

ABOUT THE AUTHOR

GG Renee Hill is an author and workshop facilitator who helps others discover and express their truths through writing. She brings her experience as a self-help memoirist and creative coach to the books, courses, and workshops she offers on her website, AlltheManyLayers.com. Through her offerings, she advocates for self-discovery and emotional awareness through writing, as she creates safe spaces for others to own their voices and tell their stories. When she's not working on her own writing projects, GG freelances as a consultant and workshop facilitator for corporate and nonprofit clients.

She is the author of four books: *The Beautiful Disruption, Wallflower, Writing the Layers,* and *Self-Care Check-In.* Originally from Pennsylvania, she now lives in Maryland with her partner and three children and can be found on Instagram and Twitter @ggreneewrites.

CPSIA information can be obtained
at www.ICGtesting.com
Printed in the USA
LVHW072224240621
690968LV00020B/61

9 781638 074212